INSIGHTS
Money

INSIGHTS

Money

What the Bible Tells Us about
Wealth and Possessions

WILLIAM BARCLAY

SAINT ANDREW PRESS
Edinburgh

First published in 2009 by
SAINT ANDREW PRESS
121 George Street
Edinburgh EH2 4YN

ISBN 978 0 7152 0885 4

British Library Cataloguing in Publication Data
A catalogue record for this book is available from the British Library

It is the Publisher's policy to only use papers that are natural and
recyclable and that have been manufactured from timber grown in
renewable, properly managed forests. All of the manufacturing
processes of the papers are expected to conform to the environmental
regulations of the country of origin.

Typeset by Waverley Typesetters, Fakenham
Printed and bound by Bell & Bain Ltd, Glasgow

Contents

Foreword

In 2008, an economic crisis convulsed the world. The comforting certainties of banking, the arcane but apparently unshakeable architecture of money and credit which had bolstered our economies and made millions of us in the west far better-off than our ancestors could have dreamed, collapsed. Just like that.

The key phrase was 'crisis of confidence'. But confidence in what? As the very foundations of the banking system trembled, one question slithered uneasily to the forefront of many minds: was it our confidence not just in banks' ability to lend, but in money itself, that had been so terribly misplaced?

William Barclay wrote his biblical commentaries decades before phrases like credit crunch and Libor rate were tripping nervously off our tongues, but you would hardly know it.

'Suppose a person's life is so arranged,' he muses, 'that happiness depends on the possession of money; suppose a recession and economic crash comes and that person wakes up to find the money gone; then, with the wealth, happiness has also gone.'

He is commenting on Jesus' powerful command not to lay up treasures on earth, 'for where your treasure is, there will your heart be also'. It is as important a reminder to governments and banks as to individual investors and borrowers that, if money becomes our god, then our well-being is on a shoogly peg.

It is immensely valuable to have so much of the New Testament thinking on wealth and possessions brought together in one volume, nimbly negotiated by such a generous and well-stocked mind as William Barclay's. To elucidate these texts, he invites us on a series of entertaining mental journeys, taking in along the way the horrors of Victorian child slavery, the poetry of Robert Burns, the magisterial Thomas Carlyle as a boy breaking open his piggy bank for a beggar, Robert Louis Stevenson being offered an omelette by his servants and the scarlet anemones blooming on the Palestinian mountainside.

Along with this capacity for colourful and telling illustration, Barclay is also not afraid to be personal. Behind the commentaries on Christ's tough, counter-cultural words on wealth, you can detect a man struggling with his own conscience. He says of the widow's mite: 'There can be few of us who read this story without shame.' He goes on to suggest that our difficulty in giving, as she did, in a way that hurts, is also symbolic of how we continually hold back in our relationship with God. 'We rarely,' he says, 'make the final sacrifice and the final surrender.'

Barclay is never afraid of a pithy phrase or even the occasional reckless generalisation. One might cavil here and there at his conclusions, but he is never less than engaging. With his scholarship worn lightly but always to the fore, he leads us towards a judicious understanding of where the New Testament stands on money, reward, labour and the correct use and status of possessions.

The possession of wealth, he notes, is not a sin but a responsibility, and people are always more important than things. Two principles which would stand the world's economies in good stead – if they only listened.

SALLY MAGNUSSON

Publisher's Introduction

One of the most famous stories in the Bible concerns a poor widow who donated the last of her pennies to the Temple. We know that Jesus told his disciples that the widow's contribution was greater than that of the wealthy people, as she gave all that she had. It's one of those stories we learn as children – so familiar that the lessons are overlooked.

William Barclay's great gift as a writer is to bring stories like this to life by explaining the fascinating detail of the story and by clearly spelling out the many lessons to be learned.

In this story, Barclay identifies three lessons. First of all, real giving must be sacrificial: it must hurt. 'It may well be a sign of the decadence of the Church and the failure of our Christianity that gifts have to be coaxed out of church people, and that often they will not give at all unless they get something back in the way of entertainment or of goods.' The second lesson to be learned is that real giving has a certain recklessness about it. The widow could have kept her last coin. 'Somehow,' writes Barclay, 'there is nearly always something we hold back. We rarely make the final sacrifice.' And the third lesson from the story is that the person praised by Jesus as the epitome of generosity was a person who gave a gift of so little monetary value: 'if we put all that we have and are at his disposal, he can do things with it and with us that are beyond our imagination.'

Readers may find the lessons in this book – on money, wealth and possessions – unsettling and shocking. They are hard-hitting lessons as they apply to our lives today. But William Barclay gives us the courage to be had from understanding the truth. Money cannot buy your character, or your relationships, or your values. *Insights: Money* certainly reveals some uncomfortable truths, but it also helps you to see life from a different perspective.

If you are inspired by Barclay's insights on money, wealth and possessions, you may wish to explore how the passages in this book are related to the rest of the New Testament. You can read more in the New Daily Study Bible series, in the following volumes: *Matthew*; *Mark*; *Luke*; *Acts*; *Corinthians*; *Timothy, Titus and Philemon*; and *James and Peter*. These volumes, and the rest of the series, are available from Saint Andrew Press.

The peril of the love of money

1 Timothy 6:9–10

Those who wish to be rich fall into temptation and a snare, and into many senseless and harmful desires for the forbidden things, desires which swamp men in a sea of ruin and total loss in time and in eternity. For the love of money is a root from which all evils spring; and some, in their reaching out after it, have been sadly led astray, and have transfixed themselves with many pains.

HERE is one of the most misquoted sayings in the Bible. Scripture does not say that *money* is the root of all evil; it says that *the love of money* is the root of all evil. This is a truth of which the great classical thinkers were as conscious as the Christian teachers. 'Love of money', said the Greek philosopher Democritus, 'is the metropolis of all evils.' Seneca speaks of 'the desire for that which does not belong to us, from which every evil of the mind springs'. 'The love of money', said the Cynic teacher Diogenes of Sinope, 'is the mother of all evils.' Philo, the Jewish writer, spoke of 'love of money which is the starting-place of the greatest transgressions of the law'. The Greek writer Athenaeus, who lived in the second century, quotes a saying: 'The belly's pleasure is the beginning and root of all evil.'

Money in itself is neither good nor bad, but the love of it may lead to evil. With it, people may selfishly serve their own desires; with it, they may answer the cry of their neighbour's need. With it, they may advance the path of wrongdoing; with it, they may make it easier for other people to live as God meant them to do. Money is not itself an evil, but it is a great responsibility. It has power for good and power for evil. What then are the special dangers involved in the love of money?

(1) The desire for money tends to be a thirst which cannot be satisfied. There was a Roman proverbial saying that wealth is like sea water; far from quenching thirst, it intensifies it. The more we get, the more we want.

(2) The desire for wealth is founded on an illusion. It is founded on the desire for security; but wealth cannot buy security. It cannot buy health, nor real love, and it cannot preserve from sorrow and from death. The security which is founded on material things is doomed to failure.

(3) The desire for money tends to make people selfish. If they are driven by the desire for wealth, it is nothing to them that someone has to lose in order that they may gain. The desire for wealth fixes people's thoughts upon self, and others become merely means or obstacles in the path to their own enrichment. True, that *need* not happen; but in fact it often *does*.

(4) Although the desire for wealth is based on the desire for security, it ends in nothing but anxiety. The more people have to keep, the more they have to lose, and the tendency is for them to be obsessed by the risk of loss. There is an old story about a peasant who performed a great service to a king, who rewarded him with a gift of much money. For a time,

the man was thrilled; but the day came when he begged the king to take back his gift, for into his life had entered the hitherto unknown worry that he might lose what he had. John Bunyan was right:

> He that is down needs fear no fall.
>   He that is low, no pride;
> He that is humble ever shall
>   Have God to be his guide.

> I am content with what I have,
>   Little be it or much;
> And, Lord, contentment still I crave,
>   Because Thou savest such.

> Fullness to such a burden is
>   That go on pilgrimage;
> Here little, and hereafter bliss,
>   Is best from age to age.

(5) The love of money may easily lead people into wrong ways of getting it, and therefore, in the end, into pain and remorse. That is true even physically. They may so drive their bodies in their passion to get that they ruin their health. They may discover too late what damage their desire has done to others and be saddled with remorse.

To seek to be independent and prudently to provide for the future is a Christian duty, but to make the love of money the driving force of life cannot ever be anything other than the most perilous of sins.

The end of the world's values

Luke 6:20–6

> Jesus lifted up his eyes upon his disciples and said, 'Happy are you poor, because yours is the kingdom of God. Happy are you who are hungry now because you will be filled. Happy are you who weep now because you will laugh. Happy are you when men will hate you and shut you off from their company and insult you and cast out your name as an evil name, for the sake of the Son of Man; for – look you – your reward in heaven will be great. Their fathers used to treat the prophets in the same way. But woe to you who are rich because you have all the comfort you are going to get. Woe to you who are filled because you will be hungry. Woe to you who laugh now because you will grieve and weep. Woe to you when all men speak well of you, for that is what your fathers used to do to the false prophets.'

LUKE's Sermon on the Plain and Matthew's Sermon on the Mount (Matthew, chapters 5–7) closely correspond. Both start with a series of beatitudes. There are differences between the versions of Matthew and Luke, but this one thing is clear – they are a series of bombshells. It may well be that we have read them so often that we have forgotten how revolutionary they are. They are quite unlike the laws which a philosopher or a typical wise man might lay down. Each one is a challenge.

As the scholar Adolf Deissmann said, 'They are spoken in an electric atmosphere. They are not quiet stars but flashes of lightning followed by a thunder of surprise and amazement.' They take the accepted standards and turn them upside down. The people whom Jesus called happy the world would call wretched; and the people Jesus called wretched the world would call happy. Just imagine anyone saying, 'Happy are the poor, and, Woe to the rich!' To talk like that is to put an end to the world's values altogether.

Where then is the key to this? It comes in verse 24. There Jesus says, 'Woe to you who are rich because you have all the comfort you are going to get.' The word Jesus uses for *have* is the word used for receiving payment in full of an account. What Jesus is saying is this, 'If you set your heart and bend your whole energies to obtain the things which the world values, you will get them – but that is all you will ever get.' In the expressive phrase, literally, you have had it! But if on the other hand you set your heart and bend all your energies to be utterly loyal to God and true to Christ, you will run into all kinds of trouble; you may by the world's standards look unhappy, but much of your payment is still to come; and it will be joy eternal.

We are here face to face with an eternal choice which begins in childhood and never ends till life ends. Will you take the easy way which yields immediate pleasure and profit? or, Will you take the hard way which yields immediate toil and sometimes suffering? Will you seize on the pleasure and the profit of the moment? or, Are you willing to look ahead and sacrifice them for the greater good? Will you concentrate on the world's rewards? or, Will you concentrate on Christ? If you take the world's way, you must abandon the values of

Christ. If you take Christ's way, you must abandon the values of the world.

Jesus had no doubt which way in the end brought happiness. It has been said that Jesus promised his disciples three things – that they would be completely fearless, absurdly happy and in constant trouble. G. K. Chesterton, whose principles constantly got him into trouble, once said, 'I like getting into hot water. It keeps you clean!' It is Jesus' teaching that the joy of heaven will amply compensate for the trouble of earth. As Paul said, 'This slight momentary affliction is preparing us for an eternal weight of glory beyond all measure' (2 Corinthians 4:17). The challenge of the beatitudes is, 'Will you be happy in the world's way, or in Christ's way?'

The punishment of the man who never noticed

Luke 16:19–31

There was a rich man who dressed habitually in purple and fine linen, and who feasted in luxury every day. A poor man, called Lazarus, was laid at his gate. He was full of ulcerated sores, and he desired to satisfy his hunger from the things which fell from the rich man's table; more, the dogs used to come and lick his sores. The poor man died, and he was carried by the angels to the bosom of Abraham. The rich man died and was buried. And in hell, being in torture, he lifted up his eyes, and from far away he saw Abraham, and Lazarus in his bosom. He called out, 'Father Abraham, have pity on me, and send Lazarus to me that he may dip the tip of his finger in water and cool my tongue, because I am in anguish in this fire.' Abraham said, 'Child, remember that you received in full your good things in your lifetime, just as Lazarus received evil things. Now he is comforted, and you are in anguish; and, besides all this, between you and us a great gulf is fixed, so that those who wish to pass from here to you cannot do so, nor can any cross from there to us.' He said, 'Well then, I ask you, father, to send him to my father's house, for I have five brothers, that he may warn them, so that they may not also come to this place of torture.' Abraham said, 'They have Moses

*and the prophets. Let them listen to them.' He said, 'No, father
Abraham; but if someone goes to them from the dead, they
will repent.' He said to them, 'If they will not listen to Moses
and the prophets, neither will they be convinced if someone
should rise from the dead.'*

THIS is a parable constructed with such consummate skill that
not one phrase is wasted. Let us look at the two characters
in it.

(1) First, there is the rich man, usually called Dives, which
is the Latin for rich. Every phrase adds something to the
luxury in which he lived. He was clothed in purple and fine
linen. That is the description of the robes of the high priests,
and such robes were hugely expensive, costing many times
the value of a working man's daily wage. He feasted in luxury
every day. The word used for feasting is the word that is used
for a gourmet feeding on exotic and costly dishes. He did
this *every day.* In so doing he definitely and positively broke
the fourth commandment. That commandment not only
forbids work on the Sabbath; it also says *six days you shall
labour* (Exodus 20:9).

In a country where the people were fortunate if they ate
meat once in the week and where they toiled for six days of
the week, Dives is a figure of indolent self-indulgence. Lazarus
was waiting for the crumbs that fell from Dives' table. In that
time there were no knives, forks or napkins. Food was eaten
with the hands and, in very wealthy houses, the hands were
cleansed by wiping them on hunks of bread, which were then
thrown away. That was what Lazarus was waiting for.

(2) Second, there is Lazarus. Strangely enough Lazarus is
the only character in any of the parables who is given a name.

The name is the Latinized form of Eleazar and means *God is my help*. He was a beggar; he was covered with ulcerated sores; and so helpless that he could not even ward off the street dogs, which pestered him.

Such is the scene in this world; then abruptly it changes to the next and there Lazarus is in glory and Dives is in torment. What was the sin of Dives? He had not ordered Lazarus to be removed from his gate. He had made no objections to his receiving the bread that was flung away from his table. He did not kick him in the passing. He was not deliberately cruel to him. The sin of Dives was that he never noticed Lazarus, that he accepted him as part of the landscape and simply thought it perfectly natural and inevitable that Lazarus should lie in pain and hunger while he wallowed in luxury. As someone said, 'It was not what Dives did that got him into jail; it was what he did not do that got him into hell.'

The sin of Dives was that he could look on the world's suffering and need and feel no answering sword of grief and pity pierce his heart; he looked at a fellow human being, hungry and in pain, and did nothing about it. His was the punishment of the man who never noticed.

It seems hard that his request that his brothers should be warned was refused. But it is the plain fact that if people possess the truth of God's word, and if, wherever they look, there is sorrow to be comforted, need to be supplied, pain to be relieved, and it moves them to no feeling and to no action, nothing will change them.

It is a terrible warning that the sin of Dives was not that he did wrong things, but that he did nothing.

The worthlessness of riches

James 5:1–3

Come now, you rich, weep and wail at the miseries which are coming upon you. Your wealth is rotten and your garments are food for moths. Your gold and silver are corroded clean through with rust; and their rust is proof to you of how worthless they are. It is a rust which will eat into your very flesh like fire. It is a treasure indeed that you have amassed for yourselves in the last days!

In the first six verses of this chapter, James has two aims – first, to show the ultimate worthlessness of all earthly riches, and, second, to show the detestable character of those who possess them. By doing this, he hopes to prevent his readers from placing all their hopes and desires on earthly things.

If you knew what you were doing, he says to the rich, you would weep and wail for the terror of the judgment that is coming upon you at the day of the Lord. The vividness of the picture is increased by the word which James uses for *to wail*. It is the verb *ololuzein*, which is onomatopoeic; that is, it carries its meaning in its very sound. It means even more than to wail; it means *to shriek*, and in the Authorized Version is often translated as *to howl*; and it depicts the frantic terror of those on whom the judgment of God has come (Isaiah 13:6, 14:31, 15:2–3, 16:7, 23:1, 23:14, 65:14; Amos 8:3). We might well say that it is the word which describes those undergoing the tortures of the damned.

All through this passage, the words are vivid and pictorial and carefully chosen. In the Middle East, there were three main sources of wealth, and James has a word for the decay of each of them. There were corn and grain. That is the wealth which becomes rotten (*sēpein*).

There were garments. In this part of the world, garments were wealth. Joseph gave changes of garments to his brothers (Genesis 45:22). It was for a beautiful mantle from Shinar that Achan brought disaster on the nation and death on himself and his family (Joshua 7:21). It was changes of garments that Samson promised to anyone who would solve his riddle (Judges 14:12). It was garments that Naaman brought as a gift to the prophet of Israel and to obtain which Gehazi sinned (2 Kings 5:5, 5:22). It was Paul's claim that he had coveted no one's money or clothing (Acts 20:33). These garments, which are so splendid, will be food for moths (*sētobrōtos*; cf. Matthew 6:19).

The climax of the world's inevitable decay comes at the end. Even their gold and silver will be rusted clean through (*katiasthai*). The point is that gold and silver do not actually rust; so James in the most vivid way is giving a warning that even the most precious and apparently most indestructible things are doomed to decay.

This rust is proof of the impermanence and ultimate valuelessness of all earthly things. More, it is a dreadful warning. The desire for these things is like a terrible rust eating into people's bodies and souls. Then comes a grim sarcasm. It is a fine treasure indeed that all who concentrate on these things are heaping up for themselves at the last. The only treasure they will possess is a consuming fire which will wipe them out.

It is James' conviction that to concentrate on material things is not only to concentrate on a decaying delusion; it is to concentrate on self-produced destruction.

The social passion of the Bible

James 5:1–3 (*contd*)

NOT even the most cursory reader of the Bible can fail to
be impressed with the social passion which blazes through
its pages. No book condemns dishonest and selfish wealth
with such searing passion as it does. The book of the
prophet Amos was called 'The Cry for Social Justice' by the
Old Testament scholar J. E. McFadyen. Amos condemns
those who store up violence and robbery in their palaces
(Amos 3:10). He condemns those who tread on the poor
and themselves have houses of hewn stone and pleasant
vineyards – which in the wrath of God they will never
enjoy (Amos 5:11). He lets loose his wrath on those who
give short weight and short measure, who buy the poor for
silver and the needy for a pair of shoes, and who palm off
on the poor the refuse of their wheat. 'I will never forget
any of their deeds', says God (Amos 8:4–7). Isaiah warns
those who build up great estates by adding house to house
and field to field (Isaiah 5:8). The sage insists that those
who trust in riches shall fall (Proverbs 11:28). Luke quotes
Jesus as saying: 'Woe to you that are rich!' (Luke 6:24). It
is only with difficulty that those who have riches enter into
the kingdom of God (Luke 18:24). Riches are a temptation
and a snare; the rich are liable to foolish and hurtful desires

which end in ruin, for the love of money is the root of all evils (1 Timothy 6:9–10).

In the intertestamental literature, there is the same note. 'Woe to you who acquire silver and gold in unrighteousness … They shall perish with their possessions, and in shame will their spirits be cast into the furnace of fire' (1 Enoch 97:8, 98:3). In the Wisdom of Solomon, there is a savage passage in which the sage makes the selfish rich speak of their own way of life as compared with that of the righteous. 'Come, therefore, let us enjoy the good things that exist; and make use of the creation to the full as in youth. Let us take our fill of costly wine and perfumes and let no flower of spring pass by us. Let us crown ourselves with rosebuds before they wither. Let none of us fail to share in our revelry; everywhere let us leave signs of enjoyment; because this is our portion, and this our lot. Let us oppress the righteous poor man; let us not spare the widow or regard the grey hairs of the aged … Let us lie in wait for the righteous man, because he is inconvenient to us and opposes our actions; he reproaches us for sins against the law, and accuses us of sins against our training' (Wisdom of Solomon 2:6–12).

One of the mysteries of social history is how the Christian religion ever came to be regarded as 'the opium of the people' or to seem an other-worldly affair. There is no book in any literature which speaks so explosively of social injustice as the Bible, nor any book which has proved so powerful a social dynamic. It does not condemn wealth as such; but there is no book which more strenuously insists on wealth's responsibility and on the perils which surround those who are abundantly blessed with this world's goods.

The way of selfishness
and its end

James 5:4–6

Look you, the pay of the reapers who reaped your estates, the pay kept back from them by you, cries against you, and the cries of those who reaped have come to the ears of the Lord of hosts. On the earth you have lived in soft luxury and played the wanton; you have fattened your hearts for the day of slaughter. You condemned, you killed the righteous man, and he does not resist you.

HERE is condemnation of selfish riches and warning of where they must end.

(1) The selfish rich have gained their wealth by injustice. The Bible is always sure that the labourer deserves to be paid (Luke 10:7; 1 Timothy 5:18). The day-labourer in Palestine lived on the very verge of starvation. His wage was small; it was impossible for him to save anything; and if the wage was withheld from him, even for a day, he and his family simply could not eat. That is why the merciful laws of Scripture again and again insist on the prompt payment of wages to the hired labourer. 'You shall not withhold the wages of poor and needy labourers ... You shall pay them their wages daily before sunset, because they are poor and their livelihood depends on them; otherwise they might cry to the Lord against you, and

you would incur guilt' (Deuteronomy 24:14–15). 'You shall not keep for yourself the wages of a labourer until morning' (Leviticus 19:13). 'Do not say to your neighbour, "Go, and come again; tomorrow I will give it" – when you have it with you' (Proverbs 3:28). 'Woe to him who builds his house by unrighteousness, and his upper rooms by injustice; who makes his neighbours work for nothing, and does not give them their wages' (Jeremiah 22:13). 'Those who oppress the hired workers in their wages' are under the judgment of God (Malachi 3:5). 'To take away a neighbour's living is to commit murder; to deprive an employee of wages is to shed blood' (Sirach 34:26–7). 'Do not keep over until the next day the wages of those who work for you, but pay them at once' (Tobit 4:14).

The law of the Bible is nothing less than the charter of the labourer. The social concern of the Bible speaks in the words of the law and of the prophets and of the sages alike. Here, it is said that the cries of the harvesters have reached the ears of the Lord of hosts! The hosts are the hosts of heaven, the stars and the heavenly powers. It is the teaching of every part of the Bible that the Lord of the universe is concerned for the rights of those who labour.

(2) The selfish rich have used their wealth selfishly. They have lived in soft luxury and lived for lust and pleasure. The word translated as *to live in soft luxury* is *truphein*. It comes from a root which means *to break down*, and it describes the soft living which in the end saps and destroys a person's moral strength. The word translated as *to play the wanton* is *spatalan*. It is a much worse word; it means to live shameless, debauched and lustful lives. It is the condemnation of the selfish rich that they have used their possessions to

gratify their own love of comfort and to satisfy their own lusts, and that they have forgotten all duty to other people.

(3) But anyone who chooses this pathway has also chosen its end. The end of specially fattened cattle is that they will be slaughtered for some feast; and those who have sought this easy luxury and selfish wantonness are like men and women who have fattened themselves for the day of judgment. The end of their pleasure is grief, and the goal of their luxury is death. Selfishness always leads to the destruction of the soul.

(4) The selfish rich have killed the unresisting righteous one. It is doubtful to whom this refers. It could be a reference to Jesus. 'You rejected the Holy and Righteous One and asked to have a murderer given to you' (Acts 3:14). Peter says that Christ suffered for our sins, the just for the unjust (1 Peter 3:18). The suffering servant of the Lord offered no resistance. He opened not his mouth and like a sheep before his shearers he was dumb (Isaiah 53:7), a passage which Peter quotes in his picture of Jesus (1 Peter 2:23). It may well be that James is saying that in their oppression of the poor and the righteous, the selfish rich have crucified Christ again. Every wound that selfishness inflicts on Christ's people is another wound inflicted on Christ.

It may be that James is thinking not especially of Jesus when he speaks about the righteous one but of the evil person's instinctive hatred of the good person. We have already quoted the passage in the Wisdom of Solomon which describes the conduct of the rich. That passage goes on:

He (the righteous man) professes to have knowledge
   of God,

and calls himself a child of the Lord.
He became to us a reproof of our thoughts;
the very sight of him is a burden to us,
because his manner of life is unlike that of others,
and his ways are strange.
We are considered by him as something base,
and he avoids our ways as unclean;
he calls the last end of the righteous happy,
and boasts that God is his father.
Let us see if his words are true,
and let us test what will happen at the end of his life;
for if the righteous man is God's child, he will help
     him
and will deliver him from the hand of his adversaries.
Let us test him with insult and torture,
so that we may find out how gentle he is,
and make trial of his forbearance.
Let us condemn him to a shameful death,
for, according to what he says, he will be protected.

                              (Wisdom of Solomon 2:13–20)

These, says the sage, are the words of those whose wickedness
has blinded them.

Alcibiades, the friend of Socrates, for all his great talents
often lived a riotous and debauched life. And there were times
when he said to Socrates: 'Socrates, I hate you, for every time
I see you, you show me what I am.' Those who are evil would
gladly eliminate the good, for they remind them of what they
are and of what they ought to be.

The true treasure

Matthew 6:19–21

> *'Do not lay up for yourselves treasures upon earth, where moth and rust destroy them, and where thieves dig through and steal. Lay up for yourselves treasures in heaven, where moth and rust do not destroy them, and where thieves do not dig through and steal. For where your treasure is, there will your heart be also.'*

In the ordinary, everyday management of life, it is simple wisdom to acquire for oneself only those things which will last. Whether we are buying clothes, or a car, or a carpet for the floor, or furniture, it is common sense to avoid shoddy goods and to buy the things which have solidity and permanence and craftsmanship built into them. That is exactly what Jesus is saying here; he is telling us to concentrate on the things which will last.

Jesus calls up three pictures from the three great sources of wealth in Palestine.

(1) He tells people to avoid the things that *the moth can destroy*.

In the Middle East, part of an individual's wealth often consisted in fine and elaborate clothes. When Gehazi, the servant of Elisha, wished to make some forbidden profit out of Naaman, after his master had cured him, he asked him for a talent of silver and *changes of clothing* (2 Kings 5:22). One of the things which tempted Achan to sin was a beautiful mantle from Shinar (Joshua 7:21).

But such things were foolish things to set the heart upon, for the moths might get at them, when they were stored away, and all their beauty and their value would be destroyed. There was no permanence about possessions like that.

(2) He tells people to avoid the things that *rust can destroy*.

The word translated as *rust* is *brōsis*. It literally means an *eating away*, but it is nowhere else used to mean *rust*. Most likely, the picture is this. In the Middle East, many individuals' wealth consisted in the corn and the grain that was stored away in great barns. But into that corn and grain there could come worms, rats and mice, until the store was polluted and destroyed. In all probability, the reference is to the way in which those and other vermin could get into a granary and eat away the grain.

There was no permanence about possessions like that.

(3) He tells people to avoid the treasures *which thieves can steal by digging through*.

The word which is used for *to dig through* – the Revised Standard Version has *break in* – is *diorussein*. In Palestine, the walls of many of the houses were made of nothing stronger than baked clay; and burglars did effect an entry by literally digging through the wall. The reference here is to someone who has hoarded in the house a little store of gold, only to find, on returning home one day, that burglars have dug through the flimsy walls and that the treasure is gone.

There is no permanence about a treasure which is at the mercy of any enterprising thief.

So Jesus warns people against three kinds of pleasures and possessions.

(1) He warns them against the pleasures which will wear out like an old suit of clothes. The finest garment in the world, moths or no moths, will in the end disintegrate. All purely physical pleasures have a way of wearing out. At each successive enjoyment of them, the thrill becomes less thrilling. It requires more of them to produce the same effect. They are like a drug which loses its initial potency and which becomes increasingly less effective. It is foolish to look for pleasure in things which are bound to offer diminishing returns.

(2) He warns against the pleasures which can be eroded away. The grain store is the inevitable prey of the marauding rats and mice which nibble and gnaw away the grain. There are certain pleasures which inevitably lose their attraction as we grow older. It may be that we become physically less able to enjoy them; it may be that as our minds mature they cease in any sense to satisfy us. In life, we should never give our hearts to the joys the years can take away; we should find our delight in the things whose thrill time is powerless to erode.

(3) He warns against the pleasures which can be stolen away. All material things are like that; not one of them is secure; and if people build their happiness on them, they are building on a most insecure basis. Suppose a person's life is so arranged that happiness depends on the possession of money; suppose a recession and economic crash comes and that person wakes up to find the money gone; then, with the wealth, happiness has also gone.

If we are wise, we will build our happiness on things which we cannot lose, things which are independent of the chances and the changes of this life.

Robert Burns wrote in 'Tam o' Shanter' of the fleeting things:

> *But pleasures are like poppies spread:*
> *You seize the flower, its bloom is shed;*
> *or like the snow falls in the river,*
> *a moment white – then melts for ever.*

Anyone whose happiness depends on things like that is doomed to disappointment. Anyone whose treasure is in things is bound to lose that treasure, for in *things* there is no permanence, and no thing lasts forever.

Treasure in heaven

Matthew 6:19–21 (*contd*)

THE Jews were very familiar with the phrase *treasure in heaven*. They identified such treasure with two things in particular.

(1) They said that the deeds of kindness which people did upon earth became their treasure in heaven.

The Jews had a famous story about a certain King Monobaz of Adiabēne who became a convert to Judaism. 'Monobaz distributed all his treasures to the poor in the year of famine. His brothers sent to him and said, "Thy fathers gathered treasures, and added to those of their fathers, but thou hast dispersed yours and theirs." He said to them, "My fathers gathered treasures for below, I have gathered treasures for above; they stored treasures in a place over which the hand of man can rule, but I have stored treasures in a place over which the hand of man cannot rule; my fathers collected treasures which bear no interest, I have gathered treasures which bear interest; my fathers gathered treasures of money, I have gathered treasures in souls; my fathers gathered treasures for others, I have gathered treasures for myself; my fathers gathered treasures in this world, I have gathered treasures for the world to come."'

Both Jesus and the Jewish Rabbis were sure that what is selfishly hoarded is lost, but that what is generously given away brings treasure in heaven.

That was also the principle of the Christian Church in the days to come. The early Church always lovingly cared for the poor, the sick, the distressed, the helpless and those for whom no one else cared. In the days of the terrible Decian persecution in Rome, the Roman authorities broke into a Christian church. They were out to loot the treasures which they believed the church to possess. The Roman prefect demanded from Laurentius, the deacon: 'Show me your treasures at once.' Laurentius pointed at the widows and orphans who were being fed, the sick who were being nursed, the poor whose needs were being supplied. 'These', he said, are the treasures of the Church.'

The Church has always believed that 'what we keep, we lose, and what we spend, we have'.

(2) The Jews always connected the phrase *treasure in heaven* with *character*. When Rabbi Yose ben Kisma was asked if he would dwell in a pagan city on condition of receiving very high pay for his services, he replied that he would not dwell anywhere except in a home of the law, 'for', he said, 'in the hour of a man's departure neither silver, nor gold, nor precious stones accompany him, but only his knowledge of the law, and his good works'. As the grim Spanish proverb has it, 'There are no pockets in a shroud.'

The only thing which we can take out of this world into the world beyond is ourselves; and the finer the self we bring, the greater our treasure in heaven will be.

(3) Jesus ends this section by stating that where a person's treasure is, that person's heart is there also. If everything

that people value and set their hearts upon is on earth, then they will have no interest in any world beyond this world; if all through their lives their eyes are on eternity, then they will evaluate lightly the things of this world. If everything which people count valuable is on this earth, then they will leave this earth reluctantly and grudgingly; if their thoughts have been directed to the world beyond, they will leave this world with gladness, because they go at last to God. Once Dr Johnson was shown round a noble castle and its grounds; when he had seen round it, he turned to his companions and said: 'These are the things which make it difficult to die.'

Jesus never said that this world was unimportant; but he said and implied over and over again that its importance is not in itself, but in that to which it leads. This world is not the end of life, it is a stage on the way; and therefore we should never lose our hearts to this world and to the things of this world. Our eyes ought to be forever fixed on the goal beyond.

The exclusive service

Matthew 6:24

> 'No man can be a slave to two owners; for either he will
> hate the one and love the other, or he will cleave to the one
> and despise the other. You cannot be a slave to God and to
> material things.'

To one brought up in the ancient world, this is an even more
vivid saying than it is to us. The Revised Standard Version
translates it: 'No one can serve two masters.' But that is not
nearly strong enough. The word which the RSV translates as
serve is *douleuein*; *doulos* is a slave, and *douleuein* means *to be
a slave to*. The word that the RSV translates as *master* is *kurios*,
and *kurios* is the word which denotes *absolute ownership*. We
get the meaning far better if we translate it: 'No man can be a
slave to two owners.'

To understand all that this means and implies, we must
remember two things about the slave in the ancient world.
First, the slave in the eyes of the law was not a person but
a thing. Slaves had absolutely no rights of their own; their
master could do with them absolutely as he liked. In the eyes
of the law, slaves were *living tools*. Their master could sell
them, beat them, throw them out and even kill them. Their

master possessed them as completely as he possessed any of his material possessions. Second, in the ancient world, slaves had literally no time which was their own. Every moment of their lives belonged to their master. Under modern conditions, people have certain hours of work, and outside these hours of work their time is their own. It is indeed often possible for people nowadays to find their real interest in life outside working hours. It is possible for someone to work in an office during the day and play the violin in an orchestra at night; and it may be that it is in the music that that person finds real life. Another person may work on a building site or in a factory during the day and run a youth club at night, and it may be that it is in the youth club that the real delight and the real expression of personality is found. But it was very different for those who were slaves. Slaves had literally no moment of time which belonged to them. Every moment belonged to their owner and was at their owner's disposal.

Here, then, is our relationship to God. In regard to God, we have no rights of our own; God must be undisputed master of our lives. We can never ask: 'What do I wish to do?' We must always ask: 'What does God wish me to do?' We have no time which is our own. We cannot sometimes say: 'I will do what God wishes me to do' and at other times say: 'I will do what I like.' As Christians, we have no time off from being Christians; there is no time when we can relax our Christian standards, as if we were off duty. A partial or a spasmodic service of God is not enough. Being a Christian is a full-time job. Nowhere in the Bible is the exclusive service which God demands more clearly set forth.

Jesus goes on to say: 'You cannot serve God and mamon.' The correct spelling is with one *m*. *Mamon* was a Hebrew word for *material possessions*. Originally, it was not a bad word at all. The Rabbis, for instance, had a saying: 'Let the *mamon* of thy neighbour be as dear to thee as thine own.' That is to say, people should regard their neighbours' material possessions as being as sacrosanct as their own. But the word *mamon* had a most curious and a most revealing history. It comes from a root which means *to entrust*; and *mamon* was that which was entrusted to a banker or to a safe deposit of some kind. *Mamon* was the wealth which was entrusted to another person for safe-keeping. But as the years went on, *mamon* came to mean not *that which is entrusted*, but *that in which people put their trust*. The end of the process was that *mamon* came to be spelled with a capital M and came to be regarded as nothing less than a god.

The history of that word shows vividly how material possessions can usurp a place in life which they were never meant to have. Originally, another person's material possessions were the things which people entrusted to others for safe-keeping; in the end, they came to be the things in which they put their trust. Surely there is no better description of a person's god than to say that it is the power in whom he or she trusts; and when people put their trust in material things, then material things have become not their support but their god.

The place of material possessions

THIS saying of Jesus is bound to turn our thoughts to the place which material possessions should have in life. At the basis of Jesus' teaching about possessions, there are three great principles.

(1) In the last analysis, *all things belong to God*. Scripture makes that abundantly clear. 'The earth is the Lord's and all that is in it, the world and those who live in it' (Psalm 24:1). 'For every wild animal of the forest is mine, the cattle on a thousand hills ... If I were hungry, I would not tell you, for the world and all that is in it is mine' (Psalm 50:10, 12).

In Jesus' teaching, it is the master who gives his servants the talents (Matthew 25:15), and the owner who gives the tenants the vineyard (Matthew 21:33). This principle has far-reaching consequences. Men and women can buy and sell things; they can to some extent alter and rearrange things; but they cannot create things. The ultimate ownership of all things belongs to God. There is nothing in this world of which we can say: 'This is mine.' Of all things, we can only say: 'This belongs to God, and God has given me the use of it.'

Therefore this basic principle of life emerges. There is nothing in this world of which anyone can say: 'This is mine, and I will therefore do what I like with it.' Of everything, we *must* say: 'This is God's, and I must use it as its owner would have it to be used.' There is a story of a city child who was taken for a day in the country. For the first time in her life, she saw a drift of bluebells. She turned to her teacher and said: 'Do you think God would mind if I picked one of his flowers?' That is the correct attitude to life and all things in the world.

(2) The second basic principle is that *people are always more important than things*. If possessions have to be acquired, if money has to be amassed, if wealth has to be accumulated at the expense of treating people as things, then all such riches are wrong. Whenever and wherever that principle is forgotten, or neglected, or defied, far-reaching disaster is certain to follow.

In Britain, we are to this day suffering in the world of industrial relationships from the fact that in the days of the Industrial Revolution people were treated as things. Sir Arthur Bryant in *English Saga* tells of some of the things which happened in those days. Children of seven and eight years of age – there is actually a case of a child of three – were employed in the mines. Some of them dragged trucks along galleries on all fours; some of them pumped out water standing knee-deep in the water for twelve hours a day; some of them, called trappers, opened and shut the ventilating doors of the shafts, and were shut into little ventilating chambers for as much as sixteen hours a day. In 1815, children were working in the mills from 5 am to 8 pm without even a Saturday half-holiday, and with half an hour off for breakfast and half an hour off for dinner. In 1833, there were 84,000 children under fourteen years of age in the factories. There is actually a case recorded in which the children whose labour was no longer required were taken to a common and turned adrift. The owners objected to the expression 'turned adrift'. They said that the children had been set at liberty. They agreed that the children might find things hard. 'They would have to beg their way or something of that sort.' In 1842, the weavers of Burnley and the miners of Staffordshire were being paid barely enough to live on. There were those who saw the criminal folly of all this. Thomas Carlyle thundered: 'If the cotton industry is founded on the bodies of rickety children, it must go; if the devil gets in your cotton mill, shut the mill.' It was pleaded that cheap labour was necessary to keep costs down. The poet Samuel Taylor Coleridge answered: 'You talk about making this article cheaper by reducing its price in the market from 8d to 6d. But suppose in so doing you have rendered your country weaker against a foreign foe; suppose you have demoralized thousands of your fellow-countrymen, and have sown discontent between one class of society and another, your article is tolerably dear, I take it, after all.'

It is perfectly true that things are very different nowadays. But there is such a thing as collective memory. Deep in the subconscious memory of people, the impression of these bad days is indelibly impressed. Whenever people are treated as things, as machines, as instruments for producing so much labour and for enriching those who employ them, then as certainly as the night follows the day, disaster follows. A nation forgets at its peril the principle that people are always more important than things.

(3) The third principle is that *wealth is always a subordinate good*. The Bible does not say that 'Money is the root of all evil'; it says that '*The love of money* is a root of all kinds of evil' (1 Timothy 6:10). It is quite possible to find in material things what someone has called 'a rival salvation'. Some people may think that, because they are wealthy, they can buy anything – that they can buy their way out of any situation. Wealth can become their measuring rod; wealth can become their one desire; wealth can become the one weapon with which they face life. If people desire material things for an honourable independence, to help their families and to do something for others, that is good; but if they desire it simply to heap pleasure upon pleasure, and to add luxury, if wealth has become the thing they live for and live by, then wealth has ceased to be a subordinate good, and has usurped the place in life which only God should occupy.

One thing emerges from all this – the possession of wealth, money and material things is not a sin, but it is a grave *responsibility*. If people own many material things, it is not so much a matter for congratulation as it is a matter for prayer, that may use them as God would want them to.

Things which cannot be bought and sold

Acts 8:14–25

When the apostles in Jerusalem heard that Samaria had received the word of God, they despatched Peter and John to them. They came down and prayed for them, so that they might receive the Holy Spirit, for as yet the Holy Spirit had fallen on no one. It was in the name of the Lord Jesus that they had been baptized. Then they laid their hands on them and they received the Holy Spirit. When Simon saw that the Holy Spirit was given through the laying on of the apostles' hands, he brought money to them and said: 'Give me too this power so that he on whom I lay my hands may receive the Holy Spirit.' Peter said to him: 'May your silver perish with you because you thought to obtain the gift of God for money; you have neither part nor lot in this matter, for your heart is not right before God. Repent of this wickedness of yours and pray God if it may be that the intention of your heart may be forgiven you. For I see that you are in the gall of bitterness and in the bond of wickedness.' Simon answered: 'Do you pray to the Lord for me, so that none of the things you spoke of may come upon me.'

So after they had borne their witness and spoken the word of God, they returned to Jerusalem, telling the good news to many villages of the Samaritans on the way.

SIMON was by no means unusual in the ancient world. There were many astrologers, fortune-tellers and magicians; and, in an age when people were easily taken in, they had a great influence and made a comfortable living. This is hardly surprising when even the twenty-first century has not risen above fortune-telling and astrology, as almost any popular newspaper or magazine can witness. It is not to be thought that Simon and his fellow practitioners were all conscious frauds. Many of them had deluded themselves before they deluded others, and believed in their own powers.

To understand what Simon was getting at, we have to understand something of the atmosphere and practice of the early Church. The coming of the Spirit upon an individual was connected with certain visible phenomena, in particular with the gift of speaking with tongues (cf. Acts 10:44–6). The person experienced an ecstasy which manifested itself in this strange phenomenon of uttering meaningless sounds. In Jewish practice, the laying on of hands was very common. With it, there was held to be a transference of certain qualities from one person to another. It is not to be thought that this represents an entirely materialistic view of the transference of the Spirit. The dominating factor was the character of the one who performed the laying on of hands. The apostles were held in such respect and even veneration that simply to feel the touch of their hands was a deeply spiritual experience. If a personal reminiscence may be allowed, I myself remember being taken to see a man who had been one of the Church's great scholars and saints. I was very young and he was very old. I was left with him for a moment or two, and in that time he laid his hands upon my head and blessed me. And throughout my life, I have continued to feel the thrill of that moment. In the early Church, the laying on of hands was like that.

Simon was impressed with the visible effects of the laying on of hands, and he tried to buy the ability to do what the apostles could do. Simon has left his name on the language, for *simony* still means the unworthy buying and selling of ecclesiastical positions and privileges. Simon had two faults.

(1) He was interested not so much in bringing the Holy Spirit to others as in the power and prestige it would bring to himself. This exaltation of self is a constant danger for preachers and teachers. It is true that they must take inspiration from being in the public eye; but it is also true – as the theologian James Denney said – that we cannot at one and the same time show that we are clever and that Christ is wonderful.

(2) Simon forgot that certain gifts are dependent on character; money cannot buy them. Again, preachers and teachers must take warning. 'Preaching is truth through personality.' To bring the Spirit to others, it is not necessary to be wealthy; it is necessary to possess the Spirit.

The place of material possessions in life

Luke 12:13–34

*One of the crowd said to Jesus, 'Teacher, tell my brother to divide
the inheritance with me.' He said to him, 'Man, who appointed me
a judge or an arbitrator over you?' He said to them, 'Watch and
guard yourself against the spirit which is always wanting more;
for even if a man has an abundance his life does not come from
his possessions.' He spoke a parable to them. 'The land', he said,
'of a rich man bore good crops. He kept thinking what he would
do. "What will I do," he said, "because I have no room to gather
in my crops?" So he said, "This is what I will do. I will pull down
my barns and I will build bigger ones, and I will gather there all
my corn and all my good things; and I will say to my soul, Soul,
you have many good things laid up for many years. Take your
rest, eat, drink and enjoy yourself." But God said to him, "Fool!
This night your soul is demanded from you; and, the things
you prepared – who will get them all?" So is he who heaps up
treasure for himself and is not rich towards God.'*

*Jesus said to his disciples, 'I therefore tell you, do not worry
about your life – about what you are to eat; nor about your
body – about what you are to wear. For your life is something
more than food, and your body than clothing. Look at the
ravens. See how they do not sow or reap; they have no*

storehouse or barn; but God feeds them. How much more
valuable are you than the birds? Which of you, by worrying
about it, can add a few days to his span of life? If, then, you
cannot do the littlest thing why worry about the other things?
Look at the lilies. See how they grow. They do not work; they
do not spin; but, I tell you, not even Solomon in all his glory
was clothed like one of these. If God so clothe the grass in the
field, which is there today and which tomorrow is cast into the
oven, how much more will he clothe you, O you of little faith?
Do not seek what you are to eat and what you are to drink;
do not be tossed about in a storm of anxiety. The peoples of
the world seek for all these things. Your Father knows that
you need them. But seek his kingdom and all these things will
be added to you. Do not fear, little flock, because it is your
Father's will to give you the kingdom. Sell your possessions
and give alms. Make yourselves purses which never grow old,
a treasure in the heavens that does not fail, where a thief does
not come near and a moth does not destroy. For where your
treasure is there your heart will also be.'

It was not uncommon for people in Palestine to take their
unsettled disputes to respected Rabbis; but Jesus refused
to be mixed up in anyone's disputes about money. But out
of that request there came to Jesus an opportunity to lay
down what his followers' attitude to material things should
be. He had something to say both to those who had an
abundant supply of material possessions and to those who
had not.

(1) To those who had an abundant supply of possessions
Jesus spoke this parable of the rich fool. Two things stand
out about this man.

(a) *He never saw beyond himself*. There is no parable which is so full of the words, I, me, my and mine. A schoolboy was once asked what parts of speech *my* and *mine* are. He answered, 'Aggressive pronouns'. The rich fool was aggressively self-centred. It was said of a self-centred young lady, 'Edith lived in a little world, bounded on the north, south, east and west by Edith.' The famous criticism was made of a self-centred person, 'There is too much ego in his cosmos.' When this man had a superfluity of goods the one thing that never entered his head was to give any away. His whole attitude was the very reverse of Christianity. Instead of denying himself he aggressively affirmed himself; instead of finding his happiness in giving he tried to conserve it by keeping.

John Wesley's rule of life was to *save* all he could and *give* all he could. When he was at Oxford he had an income of £30 a year. He lived on £28 and gave £2 away. When his income increased to £60, £90 and £120 a year, he still lived on £28 and gave the balance away. The Accountant-General for Household Plate demanded a return from him. His reply was, 'I have two silver tea spoons at London and two at Bristol. This is all the plate which I have at present; and I shall not buy any more, while so many around me want bread.'

The Romans had a proverb which said that money was like sea water; the more you drink the thirstier you become. Similarly, as long as our attitude is that of the rich fool our desire will always be to get more – and that is the reverse of the Christian way.

(b) *He never saw beyond this world*. All his plans were made on the basis of life here. There is a story of a conversation between an ambitious youth and an older man who knew life. Said the young man, 'I will learn my trade.' 'And then?' said the older man. 'I will set up in business.' 'And then?' 'I will make my fortune.' 'And then?' 'I suppose that I shall grow old and retire and live on my money.' 'And then?' 'Well, I suppose that some day I will die.' 'And then?' came the last stabbing question.

Those who never remember that there is another world are destined some day for the grimmest of grim shocks.

(2) But Jesus had something to say to those who had few possessions. In all this passage the thought which Jesus forbids is *anxious thought* or *worry*. Jesus never ordered anyone to live in a shiftless, thriftless, reckless way. What he did tell people was to do their best and then leave the rest to God. The lilies Jesus spoke of were the scarlet anemones. After one of the infrequent showers of summer rain, the mountainside would be scarlet with them; they bloomed one day and died. Wood was scarce in Palestine, and it was the dried grasses and wild flowers that were used to feed the oven fire. 'If', said Jesus, 'God looks after the birds and the flowers, how much more will he care for you?'

Jesus said, 'Seek first the kingdom of God.' God's kingdom was a state on earth in which his will was as perfectly done as it is in heaven. So Jesus is saying, 'Bend all your life to obeying God's will and rest content with that. So many people give all their effort to heap up things which in their very nature cannot last. Work for the things which last forever, things which you need not leave behind when you leave this earth, but which you can take with you.'

In Palestine, wealth was often in the form of costly raiment; the moths could get at the fine clothes and leave them ruined.

But if people clothe their souls with the garments of honour and purity and goodness, nothing on earth can injure them. If they seek the treasures of heaven, their hearts will be fixed on heaven; but if they seek the treasures of earth, their hearts will be bound to earth – and some day they must say goodbye to those things that were so precious, for, as the grim Spanish proverb has it, 'There are no pockets in a shroud.'

The two great questions about possessions

THERE are two great questions about possessions, and on the answer to these questions everything depends.

(1) *How did people gain their possessions?* Did they gain them in a way that they would be glad that Jesus Christ should see, or did they gain them in a way that they would wish to hide from Jesus Christ?

Possessions may be gained at the expense of honesty and honour. The poet and novelist George Macdonald tells of a village shopkeeper who grew very rich. Whenever he was measuring cloth, he measured it with his two thumbs inside the measure so that he always gave short measure. George Macdonald says of him: 'He took from his soul, and he put it in his siller-bag.' People can enrich their bank accounts at the expense of impoverishing their souls.

Possessions may be gained by the deliberate smashing of some weaker rival. Many people's success is founded on someone else's failure. Many have gained advancement by pushing someone else out of the way. It is hard to see how those who prosper in such a way can sleep at nights.

Possessions may be gained at the expense of still higher duties. Robertson Nicoll, the great editor, was born in a manse in the north-east of Scotland. His father had one passion, to buy and to read books. He was a minister and he never had more than £200 a year. But he amassed the greatest private library in Scotland, amounting to 17,000 books. He did not use them in his sermons; he was simply consumed to own and to read them. When he was forty, he married a girl of twenty-four. In eight years she was dead of tuberculosis; of a family of five, only two lived to be over twenty. That cancerous growth of books filled every room and every passage in the manse. It may have delighted the owner of the books, but it killed his wife and family.

There are possessions which can be acquired at too great a cost. The question we must always ask is: 'How do I acquire the things which I possess?'

(2) *How do people use their possessions*? There are various ways in which people may use the things they have acquired.

They may not use them at all. They may have the miser's acquisitiveness which delights simply in possession. Their possessions may be quite useless – and uselessness always invites disaster.

They may use them completely selfishly. It is possible to want a larger salary for no other reason than to purchase a bigger car, a new television set or a more expensive holiday. People may think of possessions simply and solely in terms of what they can do for them.

They may use them malignantly. People can use their possessions to persuade someone else to do things they have no right to do, or to sell things they have no right to sell. Many young people have been bribed or dazzled into sin by someone else's money. Wealth gives power, and corrupt people can use their possessions to corrupt others – and that the sight of God is a very terrible sin.

People may use their possessions for their own independence and for the happiness of others. It does not need great wealth to do that, for it is possible to be just as generous with £1 as with £1,000. We will not go far wrong if we use our possessions to see how much happiness we can bring to others. Paul remembered a saying of Jesus which everyone else had forgotten: 'It is more blessed to give than to receive' (Acts 20:35). It is characteristic of God to give; and if in our lives giving always ranks above receiving, we will use aright what we possess, however much or however little it may be.

The greatest gift

Mark 12:41–4

> When Jesus had sat down opposite the treasury, he was
> watching how the crowd threw their money into the treasury,
> and many rich people threw in large sums. A poor widow
> came and threw in two mites which make up half a penny.
> He called his disciples and said to them, 'This is the truth I
> tell you – this poor widow has thrown in more than all the
> people who threw money into the treasury, for all of them
> threw their contributions in out of their abundance, but she
> out of her lack has thrown in everything that she had, all she
> had to live on.'

BETWEEN the Court of the Gentiles and the Court of the
Women there was the Gate Beautiful. It may well be that
Jesus had gone to sit quietly there after the argument and the
tension of the Court of the Gentiles and the discussions in the
cloisters [see New Daily Study Bible, *Mark*]. In the Court of
the Women there were thirteen collecting boxes called 'The
Trumpets', because they were so shaped. Each of them was
for a special purpose, for instance to buy corn or wine or oil
for the sacrifices. They were for contributions for the daily
sacrifices and expenses of the Temple. Many people threw in
quite considerable contributions. Then came a widow. She

flung in two mites. The coin so called was a *lepton*, which literally means *a thin one*. It was the smallest of all coins. And yet Jesus said that her tiny contribution was greater than all the others, for the others had thrown in what they could spare easily enough and still have plenty left, while the widow had flung in everything she had.

Here is a lesson in giving:

(1) Real giving must be sacrificial. The amount of the gift never matters so much as its cost to the giver; not the size of the gift, but the sacrifice. Real generosity gives until it hurts. For many of us it is a real question if ever our giving to God's work is any sacrifice at all. Few people will do without their pleasures to give a little more to the work of God. It may well be a sign of the decadence of the Church and the failure of our Christianity that gifts have to be coaxed out of church people, and that often they will not give at all unless they get something back in the way of entertainment or of goods. There can be few of us who read this story without shame.

(2) Real giving has a certain recklessness in it. The woman might have kept one coin. It would not have been much but it would have been something, yet she gave everything she had. There is a great symbolic truth here. It is our tragedy that there is so often some part of our lives, some part of our activities, some part of ourselves which we do not give to Christ. Somehow there is nearly always something we hold back. We rarely make the final sacrifice and the final surrender.

(3) It is a strange and lovely thing that the person whom the New Testament and Jesus hand down to history as a pattern of generosity was a person who gave a gift of so little value in monetary terms. We may feel that we have not

much in the way of material gifts or personal gifts to give to Christ, but if we put all that we have and are at his disposal, he can do things with it and with us that are beyond our imaginings.

The principles of generosity

2 Corinthians 9:6–15

Further, there is this – he who sows sparingly will also reap sparingly, and he who sows bountifully will reap bountifully. Let each man give as he has decided in his heart. Let him not give as if it hurt him to give or as if it was being forced out of him, for it is the happy giver whom God loves. God can supply you with an overflowing measure of every grace, so that because in all things at all times you have all sufficiency, you may excel in every good work. As it stands written, 'He scattered his seed, he gave to the poor; his righteousness remains forever.' And in every point you will be enriched for every kind of generosity, that generosity which, through you, produces thanksgiving to God. For the ministration of this act of voluntary service not only fills up the lacks of God's dedicated people, but it also does something special for God through the many thanksgivings it produces. Through your generosity, the reality of your Christian service will be so signally proved that they will glorify God because of the way in which you obey your creed, which looks to the gospel of Christ, and because of the generous way in which you have shared with them and with all men; and they will pray for you and long for you because of the surpassing grace of God

*which is upon you. Thanks be to God for the free gift of God
he gave to us, the story of which can never be fully told.*

THIS passage gives us an outline of the principles of generous
giving.

(1) Paul insists that no one was ever the loser through
generosity. Giving is like sowing seed. Those who sow with a
sparing hand cannot hope for anything but a meagre harvest,
but those who sow with a generous hand will in due course
reap a generous return. The New Testament is an extremely
practical book, and one of its great features is that it is never
afraid of the reward motive. It never says that goodness is
all to no purpose. It never forgets that something new and
wonderful enters into the lives of the men and women who
accept God's commands as their law. But the rewards that the
New Testament envisages are never material. It promises not
the wealth of things, but the wealth of the heart and of the
spirit. What then can those who are generous expect?

(a) They will be *rich in love*. It is always true that no
one likes people who are mean, and generosity can cover a
multitude of other sins. People will always prefer the warm
heart, even though its very warmth may lead it into excesses,
to the cold correctness of the calculating spirit.

(b) They will be *rich in friends*. As the Authorized Version
has it, 'A man that has friends must show himself friendly'
(Proverbs 18:24). An unlovable person can never expect to
be loved. Those whose hearts run out to others will always
find that the hearts of others run out to them.

(c) They will be *rich in help*. The day always comes when
we need the help which others can give; and, if we have been
sparing in our help to them, the likelihood is that they will

be sparing in their help to us. The measure we have used to others will determine the measure which is given to us.

(d) They will be *rich towards God*. Jesus taught us that what we do to others we do for God, and the day will come when every time we opened our heart and hand will stand in our favour, and every time we closed them will be a witness against us.

(2) Paul insists that it is the happy giver whom God loves. Deuteronomy 15:7–11 lays down the duty of generosity to the poor, and verse 10 has it: 'Give liberally and be ungrudging when you do so.' There was a Rabbinic saying that to receive a friend with a cheerful expression and to give him nothing is better than to give him everything with a gloomy expression. Seneca said that to give with doubt and delay is almost worse than not to give at all.

Paul then quotes from Psalm 112:3, 9 – verses which he takes to be a description of the one who is good and generous. He scatters his seed, that is, he sows it not sparingly but generously; he gives to the poor; and his action is to his eternal credit and joy. Thomas Carlyle tells how, when he was a boy, a beggar came to the door. His parents were out, and he was alone in the house. On a boyish impulse, he broke into his own savings bank and gave the beggar all that was in it, and he tells us that never before or since did he know such sheer happiness as came to him in that moment. There is indeed a joy in giving.

(3) Paul insists that God can give us both the substance to give and the spirit in which to give it. In verse 8, he speaks of the all-sufficiency which God gives. The word he uses is *autarkeia*. This was a favourite Stoic word. It does not describe the sufficiency of the person who possesses all kinds

of things in abundance. It means independence. It describes the state of someone who has directed life not to amassing possessions but to eliminating needs. It describes someone who has learned to be content with very little. It is obvious that people like that will be able to give far more to others because they want so little for themselves. It is so often true that we want so much for ourselves that there is nothing left to give to others.

Not only that; it is God who can give us the spirit in which to give. The writer Robert Louis Stevenson's servants loved him. He was woken every morning with a cup of tea. On one occasion, his usual servant was off duty and another had taken over. This servant woke him not only with a cup of tea but also with a beautifully cooked omelette. Stevenson thanked him and said: 'Great is your forethought.' 'No, master,' came the reply, 'great is my love.' It is God alone who can put into our hearts the love which is the essence of the generous spirit.

But, in this passage, Paul does more. If we closely examine its thought, we see that he holds that giving does wonderful things for three different persons.

(1) It does something *for others*. (a) It relieves their need. On so many occasions, when people are nearing the end of their tether, a gift from someone else has seemed nothing less than a gift from heaven. (b) It restores their faith in human nature. It often happens that, when people are in need, they grow embittered and feel neglected. It is then that a gift shows them that love and kindness are not dead. (c) It makes them thank God. A gift in a time of need is something which brings not only our love but also God's love into the lives of others.

(2) It does something *for ourselves*. (a) It confirms that our Christianity means something. In the case of the Corinthians, that was specially important. No doubt the Jerusalem church, which was almost entirely Jewish, still regarded the Gentiles with suspicion and wondered in its heart of hearts if Christianity could be for them at all. The very fact of the gift of the Gentile churches must have guaranteed to them the reality of Gentile Christianity. If we are generous, it enables others to see that we have turned our Christianity not only into words but into deeds as well. (b) It wins us both the love and the prayers of others. What is needed in this world more than anything else is something which will link people to each other. There is nothing so precious as fellowship, and generosity is an essential step on the way to real union one with another.

(3) It does something *for God*. It makes prayers of thanksgiving go up to him. People see our good deeds and glorify not us but God. It is a tremendous thing that something we can do can turn human hearts to God, for that means that something we can do can bring joy to him.

Finally, Paul turns the thoughts of the Corinthians to the gift of God in Jesus Christ, a gift whose wonder can never be exhausted and whose story can never be fully told; and, in so doing, he says to them: 'Can you, who have been so generously treated by God, be anything else but generous to one another?'

How much do you want goodness?

Mark 10:17–22

> As Jesus was going along the road, a man came running to him and threw himself at his feet and asked him, 'Good teacher, what am I to do to inherit eternal life?' Jesus said to him, 'Why do you call me good? There is no one who is good, except one – God. You know the commandments. You must not kill, you must not commit adultery, you must not steal, you must not bear false witness, you must not defraud anyone, you must honour your father and mother.' He said to him, 'Teacher, I have kept all these from my youth.' When Jesus looked at him he loved him, and he said to him, 'You still lack one thing. Go, sell all that you have, and give it to the poor and you will have treasure in heaven. And come! Follow me!' But he was grieved at this saying, and he went away in sadness, for he had many possessions.

HERE is one of the most vivid stories in the gospels.

(1) We must note how the man came and how Jesus met him. He came running. He flung himself at Jesus' feet. There is something amazing in the sight of this rich, young aristocrat falling at the feet of the penniless prophet from Nazareth, who was on the way to being an outlaw. 'Good

teacher!' he began. And straightaway Jesus answered back, 'No flattery! Don't call me good! Keep that word for God!' It looks almost as if Jesus was trying to pour cold water on that young enthusiasm.

There is a lesson here. It is clear that this man came to Jesus in a moment of overflowing emotion. It is also clear that Jesus exercised a personal fascination over him. Jesus did two things that every evangelist and every preacher and every teacher ought to remember and to copy.

First, he said in effect, 'Stop and think! Don't get carried away by your excitement. I don't want you swept to me by a moment of emotion. Think calmly what you are doing.' Jesus was not cold-shouldering the man. He was telling him even at the very outset to count the cost.

Second, he said in effect, 'You cannot become a Christian by devotion to me. *You must look at God.*' Preaching and teaching always mean the conveying of truth through personality, and thereby lies the greatest danger of the greatest teachers. The danger is that the pupil, the scholar, the young person may form a personal attachment to the teacher or the preacher and think that it is an attachment to God. Teachers and preachers must never point to themselves. They must always point to God. There is in all true teaching a certain self-obliteration. True, we cannot keep personality and warm personal loyalty out of it altogether, and we would not if we could. But the matter must not stop there. Teachers and preachers are in the last analysis only pointers to God.

(2) Never did any story so lay down the essential Christian truth that *respectability is not enough*. Jesus quoted the commandments which were the basis of the decent

life. Without hesitation the man said he had kept them all. Note one thing – with one exception they were all negative commandments, and that one exception operated only in the family circle. In effect the man was saying, 'I never in my life did anyone any harm.' That was perfectly true. But the real question is, 'What good have you done?' And the question to this man was even more pointed, 'With all your possessions, with your wealth, with all that you could give away, what positive good have you done to others? How much have you gone out of your way to help and comfort and strengthen others as you might have done?' Respectability, on the whole, consists in *not doing things*; Christianity consists in *doing things*. That was precisely where this man – like so many of us – fell down.

(3) So Jesus confronted him with a challenge. In effect he said, 'Get out of this moral respectability. Stop looking at goodness as consisting in not doing things. Take yourself and all that you have, and spend everything on others. Then you will find true happiness in time and in eternity.' The man could not do it. He had great possessions, which it had never entered his head to give away; and when it was suggested to him, he could not. True, he had never stolen, and he had never defrauded anyone – but neither had he ever been, nor could he compel himself to be, positively and sacrificially generous.

It may be respectable never to take away from anyone. It is Christian to give to someone. In reality, Jesus was confronting this man with a basic and essential question – 'How much do you want real Christianity? Do you want it enough to give your possessions away?' And the man had to answer in effect, 'I want it – but I don't want it as much as all that.'

Robert Louis Stevenson in *The Master of Ballantrae* draws a picture of the master leaving the ancestral home of Durrisdeer for the last time. Even he is sad. He is talking to the faithful family steward. 'Ah! M'Kellar,' he said, 'Do you think I have never a regret?' 'I do not think,' said M'Kellar, 'that you could be so bad a man unless you had all the machinery for being a good one.' 'Not all,' said the master, 'not all. It is there you are in error. *The malady of not wanting.*'

It was the failing of not wanting enough which meant tragedy for the man who came running to Jesus. It is the failing from which most of us suffer. We all want goodness, but so few of us want it enough to pay the price.

Jesus, looking at him, loved him. There were many things in that look of Jesus.

(a) There was the appeal of love. Jesus was not angry with him. He loved him too much for that. It was not the look of anger but the appeal of love.

(b) There was the challenge to moral courage. It was a look which sought to pull the man out of his comfortable, respectable, settled life into the adventure of being a real Christian.

(c) It was the look of grief. And that grief was the sorest grief of all – the grief of seeing a man deliberately choose not to be what he might have been and had it in him to be.

Jesus looks at us with the appeal of love and with the challenge to have the courage of our convictions and boldly take up the Christian way. God grant that he may never have to look at us with sorrow for a loved one who refuses to be all that he or she might have been and could have been.

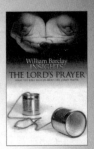

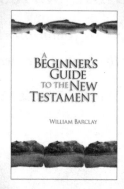